NATIONAL GEOGRAPHIC

Spiders Spin Silk

Bronwyn Tainui

Have you seen a **spider web**?
Do you know what it's made from?
It's made from **silk**.

3

Spiders spin silk with their **spinnerets**.
The silk comes out of the spinnerets as a liquid.
Then it becomes a strong thread.
Some silk is sticky.

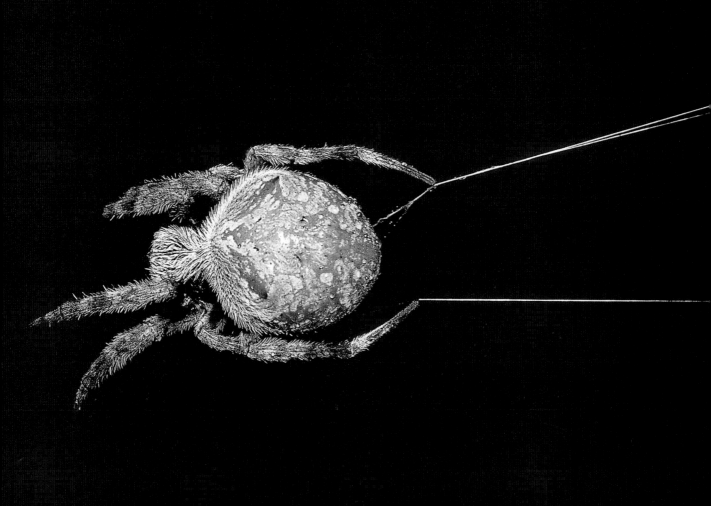

5

Spiders spin silk wherever they go.

They spin a long line of silk behind them.

This line of silk is called a **dragline**.

Spiders use their draglines to escape from danger.

Spiders can climb down their draglines
to the ground.
They can climb up their draglines
to their webs.

Some spiders swing on their draglines to catch **insects**.

Spiders spin silk to build homes.
This spider spins a silky home in a leaf.

10

This spider spins silk to line its underground home.

Spiders spin silk to build webs.
Spiders catch insects in their sticky webs.

12

Some spiders wrap the insect in silk.
The insect cannot escape.

Female spiders spin silk
to make a bag for their eggs.
The silk bag protects the spider's eggs.

14

When baby spiders hatch, they spin silk.
They spin a line of silk wherever they go.

15

Glossary

dragline — the silk thread a spider spins behind itself

insect — small animal with six legs

silk — fine soft thread made by spiders

spider — small animal with eight legs that spins silk

spider web — sticky net made by a spider

spinneret — the part of the spider's body that spins silk